THE HIGH-PERFORMANCE ATHLETE

D1364392

INSURGENT
PUBLISHING

For information, inquiries, or riffs on new editions, contact:

Insurgent Publishing
1086 Post Avenue
Holland, MI 49424
Telephone: (616) 594-0171
Email: info@insurgentpublishing.com

Ordering Information:
Quantity sales. Special discounts are available on quantity purchases
by coaches, teams, associations, and others. For details, contact the
publisher at the address above (or via email).

For Dad, who loved me unconditionally, believed in me without question, and coached me through sports and life.

You are truly missed.

PRAISE FOR THE HIGH-PERFORMANCE ATHLETE

"As an athlete, former law enforcement officer, and current special operator, the need to perform at a high level has been paramount in my life. The insights that Dr. Winkle shares in this book speak exactly to the mindset necessary to be a high level performer, on the battlefield, on the court, and in life. Learn well these lessons because in the world of special operations, performing at a high level might mean the success of the mission and the lives of your teammates."

- Special Operations Soldier (Currently Serving)

"What Dr. Winkle has done with this book is something that many trainers across the board have tried to do for eons. That is, he has taken many "intangibles" and put them on paper to preserve them for all of time. He has organized information that is crucial to ANYONE who would consider himself a high performer at anything. These are lessons that are invaluable to maxing out your potential."

- Sgt. Steve Chamness, *S.W.A.T.*

"Dr. Winkle's real life experiences with the US Military, high-performance athletic teams, and individual athletes make this book a great read for coaches and professionals in a leadership position, giving insightful examples of what young athletes need to progress not only in their sport, but in real life situations."

- James Hilvert, *Head Football Coach, Thomas More College*

"Without focus you rarely perform your best. Strangely having Dr. Winkle yell at you tends to make you gain focus rather than be distracted by the primal screams. This book has the skills, techniques and examples needed to perform your best."

- John Plasse, *Chief of Police, Sergeant Major*

"This is a must read for EVERY athlete and team. Dr. Winkle is brilliant with his words in inspiring athletes and teams to be the best by raising their standard of excellence."

- Kylie Hutson, *Team Nike & Team Pacer Professional Pole-Vaulter*

"I have known Dr. Jason Winkle personally for several years now as a mentor, coach, and friend. His book was exactly what I thought it would be—a guide for people who want to improve themselves. It is the perfect read for anyone who desires to perform at an elite level."

- Alex Bettag, *former collegiate athlete, current high school coach*

CONTENTS

ACKNOWLEDGMENTS

Years ago I attended a workshop where a very wise and seasoned coach told a story of courage. It focused on a ritual that Coach Bear Bryant used before every game. Bear would walk his quarterback down the sideline in silence until he would turn to face the young man and utter the following: "Be brave."

We all need someone who believes enough in us to remind us to be brave. That coach walking me down the sideline of life is my wife, Kirsten. Thank you for loving me and believing in me.

To my little man, Cayden, you are my reason to be brave. Putting your thoughts and words into the world is scary. There will always be those who want to make you feel small because they are unhappy or see the world differently. The words in this book are what I believe. I bare my beliefs in the hopes that you will always be brave enough to stand up for what you believe in.

I am blessed to have the best brother in the world. Thank you, Steven, for a lifetime of laughs, love, and support. I never have had to worry about someone having my back. You continue to always be there.

To all the coaches who have shared their stories and wisdom in my quest to understand high performing teams, I am so grateful. A special thanks to Ron

Prettyman, athletic director at Indiana State University, for believing in me and allowing me access to his program. Angie Lansing, Ace Hunt, Joel McMullen, John Sherman, and Dave McMannus, you are truly a high performing team. Thank you for always making me feel welcome on your turf. Thanks as well to Chris Barrett, Greg Barrett, John Barrett, Greg Lansing, Jeff Cobb, and Jim Hilvert for supporting me from the beginning. Your faith in me and your willingness to trust my player and team development program were instrumental in this book's evolution.

Thank you to all the men and women serving in the military or in law enforcement. Your service and sacrifice allow us to have the freedom to pursue our dreams. Thank you for allowing me access to your world through your stories, wisdom, and guidance.

A special thank you to COL Greg Daniels, Master of the Sword, at the United States Military Academy. Sir, I will never be able to repay you for your leadership, mentorship, and friendship. Please know that you are making a difference far beyond the walls of DPE.

Thanks to Kylie Hutson, Scott Warren, B.P. (you know who you are), Steve Chamness, Tommy Shahan, Tim Sturgess, & John Plasse for helping to make this book possible by sharing your wisdom and incite.

Finally, a very heartfelt thank you to Tom Morkes and Insurgent Publishing for all of their work in making this project possible. I couldn't have asked for a better teammate in this process. Tom, thank you for your service to our country and thanks for continuing to make a difference in the world.

FOREWORD

I've known Jason Winkle for a long time.

I'm proud to call him a friend.

I've been around great coaches, supreme motivators, inspirational speakers, tons of special people, and some of the toughest characters there have ever been. Simply put, there is no one better at knowing what it takes to be the best and actually "getting" it out of a student-athlete or team.

On numerous occasions, I've had Jason speak to my teams. I have him come to practice and evaluate us. He knows the team dynamic and what a group needs to be at its best.

I seek his counsel on a regular basis, whether it is about the good or bad in our lives, and I try to find ways he can help me get the most of out of my team.

This guy gets it.

I am more motivated than ever after every conversation I have with Jason and after every time he addresses my team. I feel rejuvenated and inspired to do my best for my players and myself.

Jason has been through plenty in his life. He has worked with the very best of our service men and women across the country as well as teams from the collegiate level to the pros.

When it comes to "High-Performance" in any field, Dr. Winkle is THE expert.

This book should be standard reading for every coach and every athlete.

I'm lucky enough to have Jason down the hall from me to be able to ask him questions on a daily basis. But now all of us have the good fortune of being able to read this book and learn from him, no matter where we are.

Greg Lansing
Head Basketball Coach
Indiana State University

INTRODUCTION

....

"Sir, are we combat ready?" he asked hesitantly.

I can't remember what lame response I fumbled through, but I clearly remember how his question made me feel.

I realized at that moment I had failed.

It is embarrassing to admit now, but that was the first time I had considered how environment and mindset impact performance. I hadn't failed in the technical or tactical realm. I was quite certain they understood how to deal with close quarters combat in a training environment. But I had failed to prepare them to deal with close quarters combat under battle conditions.

I hadn't prepared him to perform under high-stress.

It was my first trip to Hawaii and I couldn't have been more excited. I was traveling with my good friend, Jon, whom I had met my first year teaching at West Point. He was an infantry officer in the Army and a fellow combatives instructor.

We were headed to Schofield Barracks, home to the 25th Infantry Division. We were tasked with conducting a three-day Close Quarters Combat (CQC) train-up for a company of soldiers prior to their deployment into a combat zone. We were excited for the trip, yet the gravity of our charge was ever present. This would be their final CQC training before going to battle. I remember finding it difficult to sleep the night prior to our departure.

The flight to Hawaii was unremarkable other than Jon's insistence that we stay awake the entire night so we could regulate our sleep schedules following the first day of training. Frankly, I thought his idea was preposterous, but who was I to argue with a tough-as-nails Army officer who sported a Ranger Tab on his uniform. I went with his plan and, truth be told, I'm glad that I did. It made the first day a little rough, but I was able to sleep that first night with no problem and I awoke at 0430 on day two, ready to do work.

Thinking back on Jon's suggestion regarding the sleep schedule, I'm not so sure it wasn't at least partly a test for me. Jon was always testing himself physically and mentally and he enjoyed pitting himself against anyone up for the challenge. I can't help but believe that my willingness to tough it out, regardless of how insignificant it was, helped to solidify his respect for me and strengthened our friendship.

The training went like clockwork. We had made sure we were prepared.

Over prepared to be honest.

We understood the big picture and we weren't about to let those soldiers down. We had rehearsed how and what we each would teach and we had taught together enough to feel comfortable interjecting a comment or technicality when the other was demonstrating. It truly made for a well-oiled combatives train-up.

Or so I thought.

I felt great about the training right up until a young soldier, maybe 18 or 19 years old, approached me at the conclusion of the training day and asked a question that changed the trajectory of my life.

If that last sentence sounds dramatic, let me assure you that I am not exaggerating how important that moment was in how I now approach training for high-stakes events.

After directing the team leaders to get their gear squared away, I began gathering the equipment I had used earlier. As I was stuffing my gear bag, a soldier walked up to me and respectfully asked for a moment of my time. I turned to face him and was struck with the realization that something was very wrong. I have searched for years now to find the correct words to describe the look on his face, only to continually come up wanting. The best description I can muster is that his expression was one of detached fear.

The words he uttered next confirmed what I thought:

"Sir, are we combat ready?"

I left Hawaii on a mission to learn everything I could about high-stakes performance. The next five years of my life were dedicated to researching (not in a formal academic manner, but in a personal obsession kind of way) and observing every high-performing team I could find. I read everything I could find on the subject and I asked thousands of questions.

After studying various teams in the military, law enforcement, sports, and the corporate sector, I came to the realization that there existed a few common behaviors and practices that all high-performing individuals and teams exhibit. This book is a collection of the lessons I have learned on my journey since that painful day in Hawaii.

Regardless of your sport or realm of competition, my hope is that the approaches and practices contained within these pages serve to enhance your athleticism and performance, and move you forward on your path toward mastery.

To paraphrase one of my mentors, "To be great you must be disciplined."

This book will show you the way, but it is up to you to put it into practice.

STANDARDS OF EXCELLENCE

....

Perhaps we should begin our discussion about this principle by examining the only standard to which high performers aspire—*Excellence*. How you define excellence varies across professions.

Standards Matter

"Again!" he yelled. "You have fifteen minutes to get this right, gentlemen."

It was obvious to me as I sat there observing their training why the Special Weapons And Tactics (S.W.A.T.) Commander was so upset. Too many mistakes and too little focus.

"Not a good recipe for high-performance," I thought to myself.

Fifteen minutes later, almost to the second, the Commander halted the high-risk warrant training and dismissed the team. No after-action discussion or any type of critique occurred. I have to admit, I was a little surprised. And so was Nick.

Nick recently joined the S.W.A.T. team after a career in the Army Special Forces. He was one of those "high speed, low drag" type of operators that the Special Forces had a knack for developing over the course of a twenty year exposure to stress inoculation. I had only known Nick for about a year at this point through my research, but I knew him well enough to read his body language.

After gathering his gear, Nick walked by me, unable to contain his disdain and disappointment with what had just transpired.

"Can you believe that?" he asked me. "That never would have happened in the Teams (Special Forces)," his voice beginning to rise. "This isn't a joke—peoples' lives are on the line here. If we don't do this right, people could die and it's quite clear that we don't have it down yet."

I hated to admit it, but he was correct; they didn't have it down. Furthermore, by the looks of the deserted training area, the commander wasn't the only one who was more concerned about getting home for dinner than on mastering the skills at hand.

"I hate always referring to the Teams, but there were a few things that they did that we should be doing."

"Like what?" I asked.

"Like training to standard and not to time." he replied. "I understand that everyone here wants to get home to their wife and kids. We've had a long day, but I'm betting that their wives would trade a little time this evening to make sure we are as tight as possible serving one of these high risk warrants."

After some additional prodding on my end, Nick explained the key principle of training to standard that he gleaned from serving in the Teams. I want to share his lesson with you because it not only applies to high-speed tactical units but to anyone wanting to create a high-performing team.

What does excellence look like in your sport?

Every sport and every athlete will define excellence in a slightly different manner. For a quarterback, completed passes might define excellence. For a pole-vaulter, it's clearing height. For the cross-country runner, point guard, pitcher, or goalie, the definition changes yet again.

While the definition changes, there is a common theme to excellence at the team and individual level. However, the component parts aren't always easy to see or define. It

took me years of research, training, and hands on
experience to figure them out, and I'm going to share
them with you in this book. But before I do, we need to
return to Nick's lesson regarding training to standard as it
illustrates one pillar upon which excellence is built.

Conduct Your After Action Review No Matter What

The S.W.A.T. team lost an incredible opportunity to
improve because they let the clock dictate their training.

What they should have done, at a minimum, was spend
an additional thirty minutes doing an After Action Review
(AAR). An AAR is a structured approach for revisiting
any tactical event via discussion by those involved. It
looks at training from an analytical perspective that
compares *intended* versus *actual* results. An AAR is a lot
like watching film of your last competition and then
spending a few minutes dissecting what went well and
what didn't go as you had hoped. **AARs are one of the
most powerful training tools any team has in its
arsenal.**

An AAR doesn't require anything more than your
teammates and your coach. Sure, game film, 3-D
renderings of your stride, or a visual display of shots
attempted is helpful, but not required. However, to truly
benefit from an AAR, each member of the team must be
willing to be honest with themselves and their teammates

about their personal performance. They must not only be willing to take constructive criticism, but they must actively seek this type of feedback.

AARs are designed to train the athlete, operator, or businessperson, to use the power of their mind as a training tool for future performance. In an AAR, the game, training session, or business transaction is replayed in its entirety using visualization and language, first at the individual level, then collectively. Players talk their teammates through every move that they made, starting with what was supposed to happen (in an ideal situation), what they did correctly, what they failed to do, and finally, what they were thinking at the time.

Reconstructing the event using this framework helps each athlete take accountability for their unique role and its importance in the overall success of the team. Mental deconstruction of performance is designed to identify the failure points during an event (in training, competition, or otherwise) and find the correct solution for future operations. While an AAR takes additional time to conduct in the present, it saves time in the long run by preventing similar mistakes in the future.

Train to Standard

Believe me, I get it.

I understand that teams are regulated in the amount of time they can spend practicing. I actually think those restrictions are a good thing. They protect both the coach and the athlete. But they also lure us into a false belief that training to standard is not always possible in this paradigm.

Such beliefs are based on a misunderstanding of the principle. Training to standard (excellence) is not simply about physical time on task. It's much more than that. It's a mindset and an approach to training. No doubt, time on task is a large part of the equation, but it ultimately hinges on doing what is necessary to reach the standard within the constraints of your competitive world.

Let's say that you have twenty training hours a week. It's not just the hours that matter. It's what you do with those twenty hours. The S.W.A.T. team that I mentioned earlier had an eight-hour training day. The actual training that took place was closer to five hours. You don't have to be a math whiz to realize there was a great deal of wasted training time – an opportunity missed.

Be Intentional

A critical part of this training equation is ensuring that you are as focused and efficient as possible during your allotted practice time.

It begins with being intentional in how you prepare for, participate in, and recover from your training. Showing up to practice early with the right mindset establishes the tone for training. Remaining focused and present, while being open to feedback, reduces time off task. Such an approach ensures opportunities for constant learning and optimal performance. The final piece of intentional training occurs after practice, when the athlete reflects on their performance and exercises discipline in their diet and recovery regimens.

Be Deliberate

There is more to excellence than efficiency.

But you knew that already. Every high-performing athlete, coach, and leader understands the necessity of doing work outside of the official practice schedule. All great athletes do work above and beyond the standard. This doesn't mean violating the sanctioning body rules or enforcing unethical or illegal time requirements on others. It means the individual (athlete, coach, or leader) does what is necessary to reach the standard.

I'm talking about the hard work of *reflection*, *mental rehearsal*, and *self-care*.

If you accept that excellence is the only standard worth pursuing, then it won't be a leap of faith to understand that excellence requires being *deliberate*. Setting excellence as your standard means, by default, you are in it for the long haul.

Excellence isn't the one time, emotion-charged, push to victory. *Excellence is the discipline, sweat equity, and mindset that you show up with and demonstrate everyday.*

It is about winning the battle before the war is ever fought.

After Chapter Review (ACR)

1. Ask a teammate (or fellow coach) for some constructive feedback about your performance. Be an active listener as they tell you their thoughts. Don't defend yourself or explain why you did something. Just listen. Reflect on their comments.

2. Make the AAR a habit. Ask your coach or teammate what you could do better after each training session.

3. Clear your head of all your "non-sport" concerns before coming into practice or competition. They will still be there when you finish competing.

4. Ask the coach for your practice/game film. Host dinner (or BYO dinner) and watch with a teammate or your entire team.

Let it be known that anyone can constructively comment about observations of anyone's performance. Point out the "good" and the "bad" aspects of performance.

STANDARDS, TRIBES, AND EXCELLENCE

....

My beliefs about standards being a primary driver in high-performance was solidified when, as a civilian, I took a Combatives Instructor position at the United States Military Academy (USMA) at West Point.

Having worked with numerous law enforcement groups and various military personnel in a training capacity for many years, I thought my role at the USMA would be similar to the work I had done previously. I couldn't have been more wrong. My awakening began the moment I reported to the Director of Instruction in the Department of Physical Education (DPE) on my first day.

After a brief overview of departmental rules and regulations, including a confusing explanation of uniform requirements, I stood to leave. As we finished our conversation I was told, "We don't put our hands in our pockets when we are speaking to others, Jason."

"It's okay," I stated, "I'm a civilian." I was sure he had forgotten, after all I did have a high-and-tight haircut and could have passed for being in the military.

"I realize that, Jason. I'm a civilian as well, but we follow certain standards in this department, and one is that we don't put our hands in our pockets when we are speaking with others. Welcome to DPE."

I left his office wondering what I had signed up for.

In hindsight, I realize that making a big deal about a small behavior was the best thing that could have happened to me. It was important because it made me think about the "why" – why it is we do what we do; why we enforce the standards we enforce. Yet, as we embark on a quest to raise our standards, we won't always understand the "why" or necessarily see the big picture. Which is why we have to trust the process—and sometimes that means keeping our hands out of our pockets.

I quit putting my hands in my pockets that day out of fear of looking like a knucklehead civilian, but it took me much longer to understand why it was a standard of the department. The number of behavioral practices that were new to me far outpaced my learning curve. I quickly discovered, among other standards, that shirts always had to be tucked in, and the use of umbrellas was frowned upon for civilians (instead, students and teachers wore their cover, or hat, when outdoors).

There was no doubt that the officers in DPE were held to a different standard than the civilians. My respect for them made me want to narrow that gap in expectations where appropriate. I felt that I could show my respect for them by observing the "no hands in pockets," "shirt tucked in," and "no umbrella" rules. Sure it was a small gesture, but it didn't go unnoticed.

Set the Standard. Maintain the Standard.

I probably should have figured out the whole standards thing quicker, but I never did say I was a fast learner.

When I joined DPE, the offices were located in Scott Barracks, and the first thing you would see upon entering the office area was a black and gold sign that read, "Set the Standard. Maintain the Standard." I had no idea how important that mantra was to DPE, but my journey to understanding its scope and influence began with the "pocket" incident two flights of stairs above.

So when did it click for me? What was going on in my life at the moment it all became clear? I honestly don't remember the exact moment, but I can say with certainty that it occurred a few days after my first Army Physical Fitness Test (APFT for short).

Enough Isn't Enough

Each semester, all of the military officers in DPE were required to take the APFT.

Civilians were encouraged to do so as well, but not required. As my first opportunity to take the APFT drew near, I decided that I was going to take it. By this time I had learned that in the military, much like sport, your physicality is one way of demonstrating leadership.

Physical fitness is part of DPE's core values and I realized that by not only participating in, but earning the APFT Patch (an award for scoring over a certain point in each event), it would help to solidify me as a worthy and respectable member of the department. I was also in good shape, so I figured the experience could only be positive.

I knew the APFT consisted of three events: push-ups, sit-ups, and a timed two mile run, but I wasn't sure of the numbers and times I needed to earn the APFT Patch that I saw most of the officers and a few civilians wearing on

their PT uniforms.   After discovering the minimum
scores needed to earn the patch, I began my training.

On the day of the event I had my plan of attack. My goal
was to get the minimum score on each of the first two
events (the push-ups and sit-ups) that would allow me to
qualify for the patch while conserving as much energy as
possible for the two mile run. So began the APFT.

While I was doing just enough to get through the first
two events, the officers in my testing group were
destroying the standards. They were going until the last
second, knocking out every push-up or sit-up their mind
and body could deliver. I watched in awe, but I didn't say
anything or comment about their effort or toughness—I
was too worried about the next event to expend energy
telling them how impressed I was with their performance.

My plan worked. I earned my Physical Fitness Patch and
felt great about it, until the next day or so when
something dawned on me after a conversation with a
couple of the officers with whom I had taken the test.
Jokingly, I asked one of them why they went to failure on
the push-ups and sit-ups when they had obviously
completed plenty to earn the patch. From my buddy's
look alone, I knew I was about to be educated.   He
pointed out that the minimum standard was just that—
the minimum.   Furthermore, he let me know that he
knew he was capable of more than the minimum.   He

didn't want to settle for getting by. Getting by doesn't afford a sense of accomplishment or fulfillment.

Elite Groups and Extreme Standards

This is the same explanation I once heard about standards within elite teams of Coast Guard Rescue Swimmers.

You won't see a team of these guys high-fiving each other and yelling, "Congrats!" after a seven-mile, cold, open-water training swim. They know that most people in the world are not capable of doing what they do during a routine training evolution—but that's the point. For them, this sort of feat is part of the standard.

It is a small piece of the cost of entrance into an elite group.

The Coast Guard Rescue Swimmers have different standards than the general population because they have made a choice to be elite. They live and operate by a standard of excellence. They don't compare themselves to the general population. They only compare themselves with other members of their tribe. It finally made sense to me. I now understood the importance of the black and gold sign suspended at the entrance of the Department of Physical Education.

"Set the Standard" was about choice. Each of us gets to choose the standards that define us. Will it be one of minimums? Or will we be brave and choose the standard of excellence? Will we take the easy, non-risky path, or will we be brave enough to not settle for anything less than our best? I'm certain now the intent of that sign was to remind me every day that I get to make that choice. It was also a reminder that I was part of a tribe that believes it and lives it.

The Pursuit of Excellence

The second part of the puzzle, "Maintain the Standard" is a little trickier to truly understand.

At first glance it appears that standards are static. It would be easy to interpret that mantra in a manner that says, "You made it. Congrats. Now keep plugging along and don't slip backwards." But that would be an incorrect interpretation because *excellence is always a moving target*. Excellence, remember, is at least partly a performance mindset. And each time you push yourself and reach a new, higher level of performance, your standard of excellence has just shifted.

Sounds exhausting, right? It is. That is why so few athletes and teams ever reach the status of elite. It is hard work. It is a long journey that is plagued with challenges, tough decisions, and plenty of opportunities to drop the ball or not push through the finish line. All of these things are part of the journey to excellence.

What's Your Standard?

After my first APFT and the subsequent conversation, I realized that most of us are only scratching the surface of our potential.

I don't in any way mean that in a Pollyannaish, "You can do anything you decide to do," way. I don't believe that we can all, "Be like Mike." And I'm not talking about comparing ourselves to others. I mean it in a much more personal way. It's about raising our own standards and looking at our potential through a new, more empowering, lens.

Oftentimes, the tipping point for raising our personal standards is directly tied to the potential we observe in others. When you are around people who refuse to settle for anything less than their absolute best, you can't help but be inspired. There is an almost primal attraction toward that type of commitment.

We all want to be that person, but are we willing to pay the cost?

I realize now that as I waited in the push up pit, trying to catch my breath and recover before the next event, I was envious of my three teammates who were not taking the easy way out. They owned those two minutes.

They were exhausted and I wasn't.

They had discovered their truth—I hadn't.

I realized that the take away wasn't the award, pat on the back, or even the finished product; it was the standard of effort that mattered. The commitment to excellence. The sacrifice. The blood, sweat, and tears that you must pay to be the best you are capable of being.

That is what counts.

I'm quite certain that it would have taken me much longer to learn this lesson had it not been for three Army officers who, through their example, helped me understand the goal is to be an asset, not a liability. The goal is to count, not cost.

ACR

1. What are the standards to which your tribe/team subscribes?

2. What can you do to challenge your team to maintain the standards? Post a chart of weekly accomplishments? Host a physical/academic challenge for "points"?

Work with your team to find something meaningful to you and implement it.

CREATING YOUR STANDARD OF EXCELLENCE

....

Count vs. Cost

Count, not cost. It is an incredibly simple, yet powerful, way of pointing out that in every situation our actions and our words have the potential to add value or not.

We can choose to do the things that count or do the things that cost. While I received my APFT Patch that day, my attitude and my approach to cutting corners did nothing but *cost* my teammates and myself.

I cost that day because I cheated myself from enjoying the feeling of knowing that I had given everything I had to give. Nothing feels better than walking away from a challenge, win, lose, or draw, when you held nothing back.

I *cost* my teammates that day because I didn't show up and honor their efforts by paying mine as well.

We all know at some subconscious level that if we want to get better, we must surround ourselves with those who are better than us. It's the law of the performance jungle. Improvement comes faster when we are pushed out of our comfort zones by those who perform at a slightly higher level than we do.

I didn't count for my buddies. Although I couldn't perform to their level on any of the events, I could have possibly pushed them psychologically by simply giving everything I had to give. There is great power in persistence and even greater power in collective persistence. I'm sure at least one of them wanted to stop short of the whistle at one point or another, but they didn't. Or maybe they couldn't. They knew if they stopped early their buddy might not have enough personal motivation or focus to go it alone. And disappointing themselves and their teammates was simply unacceptable.

Put It on Your Mirror

In case you are wondering, I never did sew the APFT Patch onto my PT shorts. Not because I didn't earn it.

I did.

I chose not to because I was afraid of losing the lesson I had learned. I didn't want the lesson that patch represented to fade away. I figured if it was on my PT shorts, it would quickly become part of the uniform and I would soon forget it was even there.

Instead, I taped the patch to my bathroom mirror. Each morning when I would get ready for work, I would see the patch and be reminded of what it cost me and what I learned from the experience. It turned out to be a great place to put it. It was so out of context that anyone who visited my place (and used the restroom) couldn't help but ask why the patch was on the mirror.

If you had spent any time with my friends, you would know that some of the comments regarding the patch in the bathroom were quite hilarious and equally inappropriate for a book. But the benefit was that I was forced to recount the lesson over and over to anyone who asked. I became more skilled in articulating the lesson and, in the process, understood it better myself.

I encourage you to find the lesson that belongs on your bathroom mirror and put it there to remind you each day to *count*, not *cost*.

Check Your Ego at the Door

One of the key pieces of improving individual performance in any endeavor is to surround yourself with the right people.

At an early age, our parents, teachers, and coaches begin reciting this certain mantra to us: be selective of whom you give your time. Without a doubt, we are influenced by those with whom we are closest. Why then, do we rarely invest the time and effort to surround ourselves with a tribe that will empower, educate, challenge, and ultimately, make us better?

I believe part of the answer dwells in our ego. Seeking out people who believe what we believe is the cornerstone of building a tribe. But a tribe of believers doesn't necessarily help us to improve. It takes a tribe of individuals who not only believe what we believe, but also have the right mindset and skill set to push us to the next level.

Actively seeking out those who are more skilled than we are is tough to do. A bruised ego is the first manifestation of this brave act. For an athlete, this may seem like athletic suicide. You may be asking yourself, "Why on earth would I endorse this idea of seeking out a teammate that shines brighter than me? Why would I risk losing my coach's attention that I worked so hard to earn?"

Those concerns are understandable. However, they are the wrong questions to be asking. The better questions to ask are:

- "How can my teammate help me develop my skills so I can be more valuable to the team?"

- "What can I learn from working with such a skilled athlete?"

The interesting thing about both of these questions is that neither of them entails taking the easy, more comfortable way out.

These are the type of questions that actually draw quality feedback. Excellence requires that we develop a mindset that allows us to transcend our ego. It requires an ability and willingness to engage in opportunities that are developmentally scary.

There is no formula for this approach. It can be exercised in a variety of ways, specific to your team and individual needs. Sometimes it means playing in a summer league where you won't be the star because the other players are simply better than you currently are. Other times, it's choosing a workout partner during the off-season who has a stronger work ethic than you and won't allow you to cut corners or miss a scheduled workout.

Regardless of the path you choose to take in surrounding yourself with people who will challenge you, one thing is critically important:

You must work daily to check your ego at the door.

Ego is improvement's archenemy. However, defeating the ego is one of life's toughest challenges. You must be prepared to go to battle with it daily. It will rear its ugly head in a variety of forms.

Ego prevents us from being the student. Many athletes worry they will lose credibility if they ask questions or seek others' feedback. It is unfortunate that the ego has that much sway on our psyche. The only way to stretch our abilities is by continually seeking knowledge and feedback, and then acting on that feedback. Growth is optional and it always favors those willing to stand ego-less and hungry.

Separate Confidence from Ego

The destructive power of our ego really clicked with me after listening to a story about the Blue Angels. For those of you who are unfamiliar with the Blue Angels, they are the United States Navy's flight demonstration squadron. If you have been fortunate enough to see one of their shows, you already have an idea about the talent required to be one of their pilots. It's very difficult to walk away from one of their demonstrations not completely blown away.

I saw my first Blue Angels' demonstration a few months after the movie "Top Gun" hit the theaters. I knew right then and there what I wanted to be! At the time, I didn't think anything could be cooler than being the pilot of a fighter jet. Can you blame me? When I think of pilots, I can't shake the image of Maverick, a leather jacket wearing, motorcycle riding, F-14 pilot. Man, if only I wasn't terrified of flying.

I happened to run across a recorded interview of a former Commanding Officer of the Blue Angels. During the interview, he was asked a barrage of questions regarding the training required to perform at such a high level. As you would expect, their training schedule is quite rigorous.

But it was toward the end of the interview that the Commanding Officer made a comment that stuck with me ever since. He mentioned that one of the most difficult things to accomplish as a member of this squadron was to separate confidence from ego. He pointed out the importance, as a pilot, of having a high degree of confidence in your skills. However, he went on to explain how ego could be deadly.

The Blue Angels fly within a few feet of each other at very high speeds. Mistakes in their world can be disastrous. Because technical aspects of these maneuvers are important, and because the cost of mistakes is so high, the pilots rely heavily on After Action Reviews. The Commanding Officer pointed out that while they may only fly for forty minutes, their debriefing could easily last over two hours.

But it's not just the AAR that is important.

It is the mindset with which these pilots enter the AAR that makes all of the difference.

The Commanding Officer pointed out that once in the debriefing room, rank doesn't matter.

You had better be willing to take constructive criticism from the lowest ranking officer in the room if you want to get better. Those AARs are about improving. If the top pilots in the world are willing to check their egos at the door, maybe we should too.

ACR

1. Create a saying or image for your team, or yourself, to post on your mirror that reminds you to count, not cost.

2. Figure out from whom on your team you can learn. Find someone to motivate you to be better. Why did you choose him/her? What do you see in them that makes you want to push yourself to be better?

3. Challenge yourself to be confident without letting your ego stand in your way. Ask for feedback from a coach or teammate—one positive thing, one negative thing. Reflect on their comments. See the good. Celebrate it. Recognize the bad. Work to improve it.

PERFORMANCE AND HIGH-PRESSURE

....

Sometimes a shift in perspective can be life changing.

Think back to my story of conducting combatives training in Hawaii, shared in this book's introduction.

It's hard for me to believe now that I hadn't previously considered the psychological and physiological aspects of these combative skills that I taught regularly. I was a check-the-box kind of guy prior to this experience:

- Take down the weapon-wielding enemy and secure their wrists with zip ties—check.

- Execute a vehicle ambush with proper approach angles and muzzle discipline—check.

I understood the pedagogy of breaking movement skills down into bite size pieces. I had great respect for the value of repetition. And I worked hard to teach and train the skills in a manner that moved from static to dynamic with resistance.

In other words, my failure wasn't related to the type of physical skills taught or to their acquisition. I failed because I didn't prepare them to execute these skills under high-fear, high-pressure, and high-stress situations.

Nothing I taught, up to this point in my career, focused on the psychological aspects that accompany performing under fear, stress, or anxiety. That was about to change.

Characteristics of High-Performance under High-Stress

I left Hawaii on a mission.

I was determined to fill in the gaps exposed to me by that young man. I owed it to him. I owed it to all of them— every soldier that trusted me to equip them with skills that might one day save their life or someone else's life.

I took this failure hard.

I have learned a great deal since that day. Both about how to better train soldiers (or anyone asked to perform under fear, stress, or anxiety), and in how to deal with failure.

If a soldier asked me the same question today, I'd respond differently. I also wouldn't beat myself up for so long. I know now that such personal abuse does no one any good. I have since learned to forgive myself. As a civilian, I have no combat experience and no one expected me to teach like I had any. However, I should have taken it upon myself to research performance under fear and stress. And beyond that, I was surrounded by a willing audience from which I could gather real combat knowledge.

I tore into the literature surrounding combat stress and the psychology of performance, like a man possessed. I interviewed combat veterans, and took copious notes on every high performing team to which I could get access. I looked across professions. I analyzed high and low performing teams in the military, business, and sport. I wanted to know if there were characteristics, behaviors, attitudes, or actions that consistently surfaced in high performing teams that were not present in their low performing counterparts. And if so, were those variables something that could be taught and developed?

The Three External-Focused Behaviors of High Performers

It took me five years of intensive research, inquiry, and analysis, but I finally found the answer. Initially, three primary themes emerged from my observations and research. I consistently observed, in high performing groups, behavioral similarities that reinforced the literature surrounding this topic.

The three external-focused behaviors of high performers in high-pressure situations are:

1) Commitment and consistency of effort

2) Understanding of roles and their relationship to team success

3) Attention to detail

The Three Internal-Focused Practices of High Performers

In addition to the three behavioral similarities that high performing teams exhibit, I discovered three internal-focused practices. Internal-focused practices are actions that the individual exercises both privately and in the presence of their teammates. These practices, however, are primarily for the performance benefit of the individual.

The three internal-focused practices of high performers in high-pressure situations are:

1) Mental rehearsal and visualization

2) Recognizing and monitoring self-talk

3) Autogenic breathing

These behaviors focus on monitoring and directing our thoughts while using specific breathing patterns to lower our stress-induced heart rate.

All three of these practices are simple and effective and we will dive into them after addressing the three external-focused behaviors of the high performer in the next section.

ACR

1. Perform a self-assessment: what do you do that is "check the box"? (i.e. I did twenty serves. I ran three miles.) Did you really perform your best? Did you evaluate your execution? If not, go back and see how you can improve.

2. What have you done, and not performed well, for which you need to forgive yourself?

Did you miss the field goal? Did you strike out?
Did you misstep off the starting block?

Process the event. Evaluate your role and your
self-talk. Figure out how you can learn and move
on.

3. How do you embody the three external-focused
and internal-focused behaviors? Do you and your
team understand and believe in them? If not, read
the next two chapters together and discuss.

EXTERNAL FOCUS

....

I love optical illusions.

My mother bought me a book of optical illusions when I was a young boy and I remember taking it to school frequently and showing all of my friends.

I was fascinated with how something could be right in front of your face and you could miss it because you were focused elsewhere. It was almost frightening how a shift in perspective could yield such a dramatically different view.

Imagine looking at a picture of one of these illusions in which you initially see two faces, looking across at one another. But, following the suggestion that it also is a picture of a chalice, you immediately see the other object. It's easy at this point to get frustrated and question why you weren't able to see it right away, as it has now become almost impossible not to see.

Changes in perspective, however, don't always come easily. A change in focus is but one of many ways perspectives shift. Sometimes, they are the result of many years of experience and a deeper understanding of the subject at hand.

Scott Warren, a former U.S. Special Operations Command (USSOCOM) Operator, understands the value of perspective. He's been awarded medals for his valor and service including a Silver Star, Purple Heart, and four Bronze Stars.

Point is: when Scott shares his wisdom, you listen.

In the course of his military career, his understanding of close quarters battle (CQB) tactics moved from a ground-level perspective to a 50,000 foot viewpoint.

He calls this gradual shift in perspective: "Ramping Up" and "Ramping Down."

Take the tactical process of room clearing, for example. Imagine preparing to forcefully enter a residence where a bad guy has taken refuge. As your team stands outside the structure waiting for the signal to enter, you are, in essence, about to confront a "problem to be solved."

When room clearing is first taught to a soldier, he is told, "Your job is to do this and his job is to do that."

Learning this new skill is confusing and intimidating. As Scott explains, this initial "Ramping Up" phase is characterized by the new guy worrying about doing something wrong or putting his buddy in danger. It is a period where the "what if" questions are asked and discussed.

However, at some point in his military career (and the career of all elite Operators at Scott's level), Scott crossed the hump where he broke down everything he knew about room clearing and other CQB tactics into their most basic components. What initially was confusing and highly complicated became second nature. This is what Scott refers to as "Ramping Down."

"You could put a Navy SEAL, Ranger, and Delta guy in a room and we could argue tactics—do this, do that—the door opening this way. But at the end of the day, I could break it down to one simple thing: Go the opposite way as the guy in front of you, shoot the bad guys, and you will be okay," he stated.

Such a change in perspective is only achieved when you have put in substantial practice and execution time in your area of expertise.

Like Scott, I came to understand high-performing teams on a different level only after many years of research and observation of elite teams.

In the following sections, I'll show you exactly what I mean.

Inspiring Commitment

When researching, I asked members of high performing teams to describe what made them successful. They consistently shared three words that summarized their teams:

---

1) Trust

2) Respect

3) Care

High-performing teams *trust* each other, they *respect* one another and their coaches, and, ultimately, they come to *care* for each other.

An athlete is more willing to make sacrifices and consistently work hard when it involves people for whom he cares, trusts, and respects. So, if the goal is to get a team to trust, respect, and care about each other, the ultimate question should be, *"How do we facilitate the growth and development of those components?"* This is where the behaviors and practices come into play.

When coaches and veteran athletes are able to provide specific, clearly defined examples of expected behaviors that will lead to high-performance, the team is more likely to adopt them.

It's easy to forget that the psychology of influence impacts all of us—athlete or not. Telling an athlete to do something will elicit compliance most of the time. After all, most athletes trust, respect, and care for their coaches—at least on teams that work to develop such a culture. Yet while the athlete will do what is asked of him, by neglecting the "why", we are missing a wonderful opportunity to foster a deeper level of commitment (and, more dangerously, heading down a path toward noncompliance).

Taking a moment to include the "why" of the request is well worth the time investment. Such knowledge is empowering to an athlete. Every great athlete wants to get better. They know that excellence is a moving target. And when they understand the reasoning behind the techniques and training, they do more than comply—**they *commit.***

The Detrimental Side-Effects of the Low Performer

Coaches cannot successfully demand that players and teammates trust one another. Trust is time intensive, voluntary, and must be earned. The trick, then, is to quit demanding it and begin earning it.

Based on my years of observation and research of high-performance, I have come to believe that trust on an athletic team, or any team for that matter, is earned initially on **consistency of effort**.

Consistency of effort is unique to each sport, but there are commonalities across the board as well. The most fundamental of which is to:

1) Show up, and...

2) Do the work.

Unfortunately, it only takes one player cutting corners—not showing up (physically not coming to practice, or not being mentally present), and not working hard (not doing the work)—to prevent a team from reaching its potential. This problem is compounded when a player realizes she can get away with such behavior, because it encourages others to join in. Such selfish behavior erodes a team's trust. Team captains, as well as veteran athletes, must step up and address these behaviors because:

What you tolerate ultimately *becomes* the standard.

Not addressing these negative behaviors will ultimately cost your team. The hard-working, committed players on your team will eventually respond negatively. And, to be honest, their response is understandable.

The most common reaction for the hard-working, committed athlete is frustration. While most high performing athletes don't act on their frustration and inner dialogue, it does impact their attitude. A poor attitude affects performance, breeds resentment, and destroys trust.

Another common response is overworking.

When the low performer cuts corners, high performers often attempt to pick up the slack by doing both their own job and the low performer's job. The high performer recognizes the weak link and works to monitor or fix the poor performance during competition. This can be seen in all team sports. The top players try to do too much in an effort to counteract the weak link. Unfortunately, this dissipates the high performer's ability to execute their role. Thus, a weak link increases collateral damage.

The Secret to Consistently Achieving High-Performance

For an athlete or team to consistently perform at a high level, they must practice deliberate repetition. This is part of the practice of training to standard, not time.

Having a player shoot 25 free throws at the end of practice may or may not improve his free throw shooting percentage. If his mechanics are strong, the additional repetitions each day will improve his muscle memory, shooting routine, and confidence. However, if he had a flaw in his release, one that he wasn't aware existed outside of knowing his free throw percentage was in the basement, simply having him shoot free throws after practice with no feedback or coaching might actually do more damage than good.

In other words, repetition alone is not sufficient to correct problems.

That is why great coaches tell us to work on fundamentals before anything else.

I went to a small Catholic elementary school and we partnered with the other Catholic school in the city to have a youth basketball league. My dad was asked to coach in this league in addition to his other coaching job.

The fourth, fifth, and sixth grade season began and my dad was perpetually angry with me for my half-court trick shot obsession. I got lectured and scolded, but it didn't help. Every day, I'd work on my trick shots and ignore the boring fundamentals like free throws and layups.

During the last game of the season, as the clock ticked down and we were down by two points, I intercepted a pass. I took off sprinting toward our basket with no one even close to me. I came in at full speed and…

I missed the basket.

In the silence of the small gym, where the bleachers stop six inches from the baseline and the Saint Mary's logo was too big for the undersized gym floor, my father's thunderous voice boomed, "A simple damn layup!"

My mother was horrified; I was embarrassed; my dad was furious; and my brother and teammates were laughing hysterically.

Lesson learned.

After that, I worked on my fundamentals and I practiced until I knew that I wouldn't miss another wide-open layup—ever. The half court shots would have to wait until coach left the court.

Twenty-five years later, those words that echoed off the gymnasium walls of my youth were being repeated to me by a high-speed S.W.A.T. Commander. For three days, I watched the Advanced S.W.A.T. course being delivered and I would bother the instructors constantly with questions about high-performance and executing under high-stress. At one point during the training, I caught the commander of the unit sitting alone, watching his team do repetition after repetition of the same room-clearing scenario.

In the more than two decades he spent as a S.W.A.T. operator, he shared that the teams that he felt were the most dialed-in (S.W.A.T. talk for very skilled technically and tactically) were the ones that figured out how to get past the monotony of doing repetition after repetition. I shared with him one of my favorite quotes, "Repetition is the mother of all skills."

His response: "That's true, so you better be doing every repetition with intention and correct technique."

How to Build Respect in a High-Performance Team

Spend some time watching high-performing teams practice and you will constantly hear respect being mentioned and demonstrated. Self-respect. Respect for your teammates, your coach, your school, and your opponents. Respect for the game. Like trust, there is more than one way to develop respect on a team.

I have come to believe that a great starting point for building respect is to help each player understand that she has a particular role to play. Furthermore, it is critical that she understand that executing her role to the best of her ability is paramount to the overall success of the team.

Understanding and executing your role to the best of your ability fosters respect on a team; it demonstrates a commitment to improve the team via each athlete's training and sacrifice. Respect is further developed when a coach or veteran athlete explains, in clear terms, how each role, regardless of how insignificant it appears, is essential for the team's success.

I love sharing the approach elite S.W.A.T. teams use to reinforce the importance of each person's role in executing the mission. If you were to watch one of these high-performing teams (unlike the one S.W.A.T. team we discussed earlier) prepare to serve a high-risk warrant, you would quickly see how important this approach is to operational success.

Before heading to the location where they will serve the warrant, the entire team reviews the operation plan. Each member of the team will then verbally tell their teammates what they will be doing during the warrant execution, including all areas of their personal responsibility. The team leader would facilitate this pre-mission drill by asking each teammate to report out.

For example, "Breacher, report out."

The breacher would then state, "My responsibility is to gain entry for the team into the specified residence. I will approach the residence in the number two spot from the Alpha staging area. Once we are staged on the east side of the front door, I will use a breaching ram to gain entry at the primary access point. If entry cannot be attained at the primary point, I will use the adjacent window as my secondary entry point."

This drill would be repeated until everyone on the team verbally described his or her area of responsibility. It becomes crystal clear how important it is for everyone to execute their role to the best of their ability. Such a process lessens confusion about who is responsible for what.

I have heard the same concept expressed in a different manner from a retired Special Operations Team Leader. He shared that everyone on his team worked for the intelligence guy, until radio silence. Everyone worked for the sniper, until the shot was taken. Everyone worked for the breacher, until the door was blown. I'm sure you get the picture. Sharing these anecdotes with you reminded me of a quote I ran across years ago and continue to use today when I speak to teams across the country:

"The strength of the wolf is the pack and the strength of the pack is the wolf."

This idea applies to all team sports. From traditional team sports, such as football or softball, to sports such as cross country, wrestling, or swimming, where you compete in various capacities as an individual, but your outcome is figured into the collective win or loss, each athlete has a critical role to play that extends beyond their individual performance. Each athlete, regardless of their playing status, has a role that they must own for the team to achieve sustainable high-performance.

A starter's primary role is to show up every day and lead by example. Starters are expected to work hard, be respectful, and continue to earn the starting position each day in practice. A backup's role is to work to become a starter. Know your position, support the starter, be respectful of the coach's decision, and be ready to get in the game. An injured player's role is to stay involved with the team—remain engaged, religiously execute the assigned rehabilitation exercises, and support teammates, especially the teammate who is now playing your position.

A deep backup (someone who knows they won't see playing time during the season) has a unique and important role to play in the team's success. Their job is to support their teammates by cheering and challenging them in practice as well as learning the game and the coach's expectations.

Athletes who own their role and execute it to the best of their ability tend to avoid a negative behavior into which many others fall. I constantly witness athletes on the sidelines of games complaining about not getting playing time. The statement, "I can't believe coach thinks that guy's better than me. I can school that guy!" is heard on every sideline of every mediocre team in the country.

The problem with such statements, outside of being disrespectful to their teammate and coach, is that these athletes are destroying any chance they might have to improve their current situation.

Think of it this way: I am a coach and I have two very good players that are only slightly less talented than my starter. One of them constantly gripes about not getting playing time while the other one, who wants to play just as badly as his bench-warming buddy, is very supportive of his teammates, has a positive attitude, and stays engaged in the game. Which one will I choose if my starter is injured?

That's a no brainer, right? Then why do we see such negative behaviors all the time on the sidelines? I think it's because we don't stress enough one of the key laws of life that states, "In sport, like life, performance is rewarded." So, if you want to have the best chance of changing your role in the future, make sure you execute your current role to the best of your ability.

Whether it's being the best backup or most vocal cheerleader for your teammates, **own your role so that there is no doubt that you count, not cost.**

The Importance of Caring in High-Performance

High-performing teams care about each other.

That doesn't mean that they don't argue or that they always agree. Complete harmony is not realistic or completely desirable if you want to grow as a person or a team. Growth requires that we put ourselves in situations that stretch us mentally, physically, and emotionally. Think of it in these terms, "If you continue to do what you have always done, you will get what you have always gotten."

Growth only occurs outside of our comfort zone.

Having a team comprised of individuals who care about each other is critical if you want athletes to feel confident and supported in stretching their current skill sets. It is easier to take the risks that true growth requires when surrounded by people who care about us and want us to succeed.

Similar to trust and respect, caring about someone can't be mandated. Perhaps that is why so many teams fall short of high-performance. Caring can't be faked either, at least not for long. It needs to be nurtured and, therefore, takes commitment of time and effort. However, coaches and athletes can behave in certain ways that will increase the likelihood of athletes investing in one another. Eventually, these investments of time and attention ultimately encourage athletes to rely on each other and to care for one another.

Applying the GPS Theory to High-Performance

When it comes to facilitating a team culture that embraces players caring about one another, I default to my "GPS Theory."

Early one morning, I was sitting in my car plugging an address into my GPS as I contemplated the talk I was scheduled to give later that day. As I waited for the GPS to calculate my route, I caught myself thinking about the topic on which the coach had asked me to speak—team cohesion. She felt as though her athletes only cared about their individual performance. She was hoping I could share some thoughts with them to change their behavior.

I was shaken from my thoughts by the familiar "beep" of my GPS, alerting me that my route was planned. As I peered at the multiple routes presented, it dawned on me—the coach needed to take what seemed to be a circuitous route to achieve her goal. My GPS pointed out in clear terms that the shortest distance route was not the optimal route considering the construction that was present. The best route to get to my destination that day was to drive a little out of the way, ultimately saving time and frustration.

This is the GPS Theory: **the shortest route is not always the best path.**

To reach her goal, she would have to employ a long-term approach, skipping the "instant gratification" route and sticking with a longer, more complex process, which would ultimately get to the end product in a more desirable manner. From my earlier research, I gleaned that high-performing teams care about each other and one means of achieving such an end state was to teach athletes to pay attention to details. I realize this approach requires a little explanation.

The practice of paying attention to details begins with an assumption. It assumes that things are done for a reason and that in high-performance, it is the small things that separate the good from the great. There is no chance for the small things to even be addressed if we are not aware of them. The journey toward awareness often begins at a very surface and self-centered level.

The athlete realizes that, in order to play or get better, faster, or stronger, they must not ignore the details. They, for selfish reasons initially, realize that cutting corners in drills or not upholding the team's standards will impact their playing time. It begins with the little things. Keeping jerseys tucked in, running through the finish line, or sitting in the front row of all of your classes are examples of things coaches may request. Each one of these actions requires self-discipline.

Eventually, great athletes will come to understand that self-discipline is the doorway to mastery of any discipline. Your sport and your academic career are the disciplines of this phase of your life. As you move through life, however, self-discipline will continue to positively impact your quality of life. It will improve your career, make you a better spouse and parent, and allow you to achieve the goals you set.

Paying attention to details is a function of self-discipline. Exercising this discipline not only improves you, it has the power to improve others as well. While the practice of self-discipline is often inwardly focused initially, it has the potential to grow into a wonderful externally focused practice. If your personal or team standard is excellence, you quickly learn that it can only be attained consistently by exercising self-discipline, in the practice of paying attention to details.

The self-disciplined athletes, those that have held themselves accountable to the standard begin to take notice of their teammates' choices and efforts. Usually the first outgrowth of this transition is that the team begins to police itself. Teammates that cut corners or don't uphold the team standards are called out and positive peer pressure is applied to get them to comply, to be better.

This internal policing by the athletes usually signifies a shift in culture taking place. These transitional periods usually feel unstable and uncomfortable to both the athletes and the coaches, but they are a necessary part of moving a team to a higher level of functioning. If these calls for accountability are done in a respectful and professional manner, they will eventually morph again into something even more positive.

Think of those just described tumultuous times as the additional back roads, full of curves and stoplights, which our GPS advised us to take.

Was it an easy route?

No way.

But in the long run, it was the better route to follow. I have witnessed this evolution on numerous teams of all disciplines over the years. The common outgrowth of this transition is that athletes begin to notice things other than standard violations; they begin to look caringly at one another. An emotional event in a teammate's life, that would have gone unnoticed previously, is recognized and addressed with personal support. Athletes notice when one of their teammates is struggling in the classroom and they address the problem by offering to tutor or simply study with them. The teammate that is not focused is gently confronted.

Those that are cutting corners or not upholding the team's standards are approached by their teammates and policed into changing their behaviors, or they leave on their own accord.

Paying attention to details and having self-discipline increase emotional intelligence (EQ) individually and collectively. EQ deals with a person's ability to accurately recognize their emotions and use that knowledge to develop their relationships. Athletes with high EQ connect easier and at deeper levels than those with low EQ.

The GPS Theory holds that the shortest route to your goal is not always the most valuable or the best long term approach, especially when it comes to building a team of athletes who care about each other.

Real Time Excellence

One of the greatest, and most consistent, displays of external-focused behaviors that I have witnessed is by the artists who perform STOMP. Five minutes into the performance, you realize these performers are not only percussionists, they are athletes. They jump, spin, climb, and dance while playing together in perfect rhythm using a variety of makeshift instruments. They use hubcaps, buckets, brooms, and basketballs among other things to create a perfectly synced movement and sound experience.

Do they trust each other? Without a doubt. All you have to do is watch how they interact with one another. They throw things to each other without looking; their timing is impeccable. They laugh, dance and swing sticks at each other, sometimes from blind angles. Yes, I completely believe they trust each other. I also believe that their trust is at least partly the outgrowth of the **consistency of effort** that is required to do anything at such a high level. That type of time on task builds trust.

These performers own their roles. It is obvious that each person on stage is a master of his or her realm. At some point in their career, each one of them has learned how to get beyond the monotony of high repetitions. The precision and timing involved in their performance is a testament that they understand each piece of the high-performance equation.

There are a thousand places in each performance where lack of attention to details would impact the flow and quality of the moment, but those mistakes rarely happen.

It is quite clear that they subscribe to a standard of excellence. It is also very apparent that they care about each other and they love what they do.

ACR

1. Do you focus on something so much that you become obsessed? Your weight? Your one rep max? Your grade on a test?

Challenge yourself to look beyond and see the bigger picture. What can you learn from taking in the details or focusing on more than that one aspect?

2. Trust, respect, and care: how do you demonstrate each of them on your team? Where can you improve?

3. Do you provide consistency in your effort? Can your teammates count on you daily?

4. Do you understand and execute your role to your best ability? On the court? In the classroom? For your family?

5. How can you show that you care about your teammates? Make it authentic—don't do something fake to prove a point.

INTERNAL FOCUS

....

In the last section, we discussed three powerful external-focused behaviors that emphasize interactions with teammates.

Athletes who show up every day with a strong work ethic stand out from their peers. And any athlete who owns her role and pays attention to details will be noticed. These behaviors get a great deal of talk time and attention from coaches because they are observable, relatively easy to explain, and incredibly important to high-performance.

The next section will address internal-focused practices that athletes can exercise alone or in the presence of their teammates. These actions focus primarily on the individual athlete's development. They include: mental rehearsal and visualization, monitoring self-talk, and the practice of autogenic breathing.

Visualizing the Jump

"Hell Yeah!" she exclaimed as she looked at the bar still perched fifteen feet, seven inches above her.

It was the third best women's indoor vault in American history.

Her fists pumped in excitement and she was greeted with a sea of high-fives. The tears began to flow.

Kylie Hutson is a professional pole-vaulter and one of the most mentally tough athletes I know.

She has to be.

When you get into the thin air in which she competes, mental resilience and discipline are mandatory.

Everything about the morning of the 2013 USATF Indoor Nationals just felt right to Kylie. The night before the competition, she did what she always does—she visualized every jump she would make the next day. By this point, she had seen this competition so many times in her mind that she was incredibly confident.

Her actions on the day of the event were ritualistic. She began her warm up with running drills followed by her standard relaxation technique of propping her legs up on a bench and listening to music. Later she would execute her vaulting drills—performed in the same manner as she has done a million times before.

She would get up and move around every ten minutes until it was close to her time to jump. "The first jump is always a little nerve racking and I'm usually a little hesitant, but that day I just felt like everything was right."

She felt so good that she chose to open at fourteen feet, five inches—her highest opening jump to that point. After executing her autogenic breathing she began her self-talk cues: "See it. Take it to the top. Be big." Then she rocked back and took off toward the pit where she cleared the height easily.

Her ritual of legs up, visualizing the next jump, autogenic breathing, and positive self-talk cues were repeated between each vault. Everything went like clockwork until she missed her first two attempts at fifteen feet, five inches. Some athletes panic in moments like this.

Kylie simply changed her self-talk: "Trust yourself."

She cleared the height on her third attempt.

When she vaulted at fifteen feet, seven inches, she was the only competitor to be found. This meant she only had three minutes between jumps.

Instead of letting the pressure crush her, Kylie sat on the bench, visualized the jump, and began her self-talk, just like before.

She ended the day with a new personal record on her third attempt and a second place finish at the USATF Indoor Nationals.

Developing a Routine of Mental Rehearsal and Visualization

I was first introduced to visualization by a close friend who coached high school baseball. He was a firm believer in its value. During pre-game warm up, he would have his team take their positions on the field and close their eyes and visualize how they would respond to the various scenarios he would call out.

I was surprised initially that he believed such an exercise was worth the time it took to execute. But after watching the team warm up with this exercise and then respond, almost instinctively, to similar situations during a game, I became a believer. I spoke on numerous occasions with his athletes about this approach to visualization. Most of his athletes shared that this routine increased their confidence going into each game.

Sport psychologists have professed the benefits of visualization and mental rehearsal for many years. Its use is often recommended when an athlete has made a small adjustment in a particular technique and needs to rehearse it to build confidence. Furthermore, athletes are commonly encouraged to use visualization for the maintenance of performance levels, as preparation for specific games and opponents, and upon returning to play after an injury.

Visualization in Action

As a Player Development Specialist, I have worked with many athletes who have come to appreciate the power of visualization.

Chris became a believer, but only after he hit bottom.

He looked up at the scoreboard; 4:15 left in the game. The score was tied and the starting quarterback was still on the turf with three athletic trainers huddled around him.

"This isn't good," thought Chris.

Chris was the backup quarterback and hadn't taken a single snap during a game this season. As he watched the scene unfold, the butterflies in his stomach seemed to be increasing. Chris knew that shortly he would be called into the game. In a moment of panic he realized that he didn't know where he had placed his helmet. To make matters worse, he wasn't warmed up.

The coach grabbed Chris by the shoulder as his teammate handed him the missing helmet. "Take us home, Chris," shouted the coach as Chris ran onto the field. He was visibly shaking as he entered the huddle to call the next play.

Chris choked and his team lost.

The bigger problem, however, was lurking a week away (play suspense music here)—the local rivalry game. It's the biggest game of the year. Win that game and the hometown views it as a winning season, regardless of the overall win/loss record. Yeah, it's that big of a deal. Chris saw this as a way to redeem himself and his horrific performance the past Friday. If he could come out and win this game, he knew his past performance would quickly be forgotten. That glimmer of hope, however, was quickly extinguished by the added pressure that Chris had now piled on his plate.

Luckily for Chris, his coach understood the power of visualization in building confidence. All week long, after practice, Chris sat in the coach's office and was guided through visualization exercises. He closed his eyes and his coach gave him a scenario that they most likely would face Friday. Chris visualized the defense and then verbally walked his coach through each play he called. He took his time forming the image in his mind, making it as detailed and lifelike as possible. Chris was taught this process increased in value in proportion to the detail in which he could visualize the events.

Hundreds of physical repetitions and even more mental repetitions later, Chris took the field with confidence. He knew that he was ready for the game. He had paid his dues and he took comfort in the words of wisdom his coach offered him right before exiting the locker room.

"Remember, Chris, this is the first time the opposing defense has seen you. But you have gone to battle with them hundreds of times this week—and you dominated them each and every time."

Sun Tzu, one of the greatest strategists of all time once said, "The ideal general wins the war before the battle is ever fought." Visualization allows you to be the general.

Now all you have to do is execute your plan.

Change Your Thoughts, Change Your Performance

Several years ago, a colleague introduced me to a computer science concept called GIGO, or "garbage in, garbage out."

It refers to computers processing, without question, bad data (nonsensical input) and producing nonsensical output. In other words, the quality of input equals the quality of output. The parallel to high-performance athletes is unmistakable.

It is commonly believed that each of us has roughly 50,000 thoughts a day. That is a lot of mental repetitions. Depending on the quality of our thoughts, those 50,000 repetitions can create the life we've always dreamed of or create a nightmare we want to escape. Unfortunately, most of our thoughts and self-talk are, at best, disempowering.

Our brains have an incredible capacity to solve the problems we present to it, both consciously and unconsciously. This means the brain is always working to give us answers to our internal dialogue or self-talk (whether we're looking for answers or not). If our internal dialogue is negative (garbage in), the output will be negative (garbage out).

Kelli, like so many other athletes I have worked with, struggled with her transition from high school to college play. As a freshmen on a Division I basketball team, she struggled with her internal dialogue her entire first year. After a dominating high school senior season, she was given an athletic scholarship to attend college. In the course of one year, she went from star player on her high school team to competing for (and losing) a starting position on her college team. Her self-talk was hurting her performance and she had no idea.

Kelli would be on the sideline watching her teammate in the starting role and her self-talk would kick in. "Why can't I just relax and play like I know how when I get in there? Why do I tense up and blow every chance I get to shine?"

Garbage in.

So Kelli's brain went to work. Her statements were being supported with a rich collection of unconscious answers and data. Her next round of self-talk included the following as her brain supplied supporting documentation:

"I've always clinched up under pressure. I've never played well in these situations. With all the pressure I've put on myself to perform now, I might as well forget ever starting this season. I'll never make it on this team unless I figure out how to not choke when the pressure is on."

Garbage out.

Breaking this cycle of negativity takes work, but it is possible. It begins with first monitoring your self-talk and then short-circuiting the negative thoughts by dismissing them and replacing them with positive ones. Once Kelli was aware of her self-talk, she rerouted her feelings of insecurity in a more positive manner by asking a different question. "What can I do to make sure I perform my best when I get the chance?"

This question resulted in her brain delivering a completely different set of responses than the negative questions produced. Her self-talk changed to:

"I can do this. All I have to do is breathe."

Occasionally she would substitute the mantra, "Put the time in. Do your reps, and remember, you have done this a million times before."

When it comes to high-performance, we're at the mercy of our inputs.

Just like a computer: Garbage In, Garbage Out.

When we change the questions we feed to our internal dialogue, our output changes. If you want a better answer, you need to ask a better question. How we frame our self-talk plays a significant role in our attitude, our actions, and our success. Another key outcome of a positive and intentional question, either out loud or in the chatter of our own psyche, is that it directs our focus.

Focus = Reality

Questions matter because they focus our attention. What we focus on becomes our reality.

I'm a motorcycle fanatic. I grew up around motorcycles and I cherish those beautiful fall days where I can get out on the road for a few hours and ride.

My fascination with motorcycles evolved into a love of racing as well. I especially enjoy watching the Superbikes rip around hairpin curves at 180 miles per hour. It's one thing to talk about high speed and quite another to see it firsthand. Watching them at track level zip past you leaves your head spinning in awe and envy at the talent of these professional racers.

Occasionally, you come across a powerful life lesson in an unlikely place. A friend of mine told me about such a situation he experienced. It was the first time he had ever attended a Superbike Racing School, and he was introduced to one of those lessons about high-performance. These racing schools are designed for the recreational rider to the serious racer-wanna-be. They run for one to two days and teach everything from general track rules, common rider errors, turn entry speed, cornering, high speed bike stability, performance shifting, to choosing passing lines.

He told me, "Sitting in the classroom, it's tempting to let your mind wander as the instructor covers rule after rule about track safety. After all, I came here to learn how to push my bike and my skills to the limit—not sit in a classroom all day." The track called, but completing the lecture portion is non-negotiable.

"Just when you think you can't take any more discussion about the importance of finding and protecting your line on the track," he recalls, "the instructor said something that snapped me out of my daze. I sat up in my chair as he finished his lesson on high speed cornering."

"At some point over the course of the next day and a half," the instructor explained, "you will go into a corner too hot (meaning too fast) and you will feel the bike floating to the outside of the corner. It will feel like your bike is being pulled toward the wall or guardrail. It is here where you, as a rider, must do something that goes against human nature."

"You must resist the urge to look at the wall."

With his hand, he demonstrated the bike floating toward the outside wall of a corner. My friend explained that if you look at the wall, where you don't want to end up, the geometry of the bike is altered. It stands the bike more upright and your trip into the wall is actually accelerated. Not good.

He went on to say that the trick is to look through the corner to where you ultimately want to end up. Using the same hand motion he eloquently demonstrates how looking through the corner again would change the bike's geometry. It puts the bike on the maximal amount of lean it can carry, which will pull you out of the corner and away from the wall.

As I stood there listening to him, I realized: that is not just a racing lesson—it's a life lesson on high-performance.

Don't focus on where you don't want to be—focus on where you want to go.

A change in focus changes everything. And perhaps the most empowering part of this lesson is that we get to choose what we focus on. *It's our choice.* It may not always be as easy as the instructor noted in his lesson. Sometimes it may even go against human nature. But those pro Superbike racers prove it is possible every time they whip though one of those hairpin curves successfully.

Shake It Off / Refocus

It happened.

It always does at some point in the season. An infielder bobbled a routine ground ball and was charged with an error.

In my role as a Player Development Specialist, I don't worry about the error; I worry about what happens immediately after the error. And it happened. Immediately the player's posture changed. She visibly pouted and everyone could see that she was very angry with herself.

The disappointment is understandable. Many athletes put incredible amounts of pressure and unrealistic expectations on themselves. When things don't go as they hoped or they make a mistake that they can't shake off, there is a great deal of collateral damage that often follows.

The ability to shake off a mistake and refocus is a skill that an athlete must master if they ever hope to be a high performer.

It's one thing to drop your head for a moment to quickly learn from the mistake and regroup, and it's quite another to not let it go. An athlete that continually pouts about a mistake is not actively working toward getting back in the moment. She's selfishly reliving the mistake and beating herself up mentally – and this *costs* the rest of the team.

Internal dialogue affects external performance.

A player that is visibly upset is, almost without fail, mentally talking herself out of the next play and out of any chance for high-performance in the current game.

As I stood watching this player self-destruct, I couldn't help but think of the following quote:

"If you face but one opponent and doubt yourself, you are already outnumbered."

She bobbled the ground ball. There was nothing she could do to change it. She had to move on. She needed to monitor her self-talk so that it wouldn't do additional damage (to herself and her team). This might seem easier said than done, but there's actually a simple technique for getting our mind back in the game (or on the battlefield or in the boardroom) after a mistake.

Focus on What You Can Control

As much as this player would have loved to travel back in time and change her mistake, she could not. What she could do, however, is focus on the things she can control – right now.

She can control how she responds to the disappointment. She can focus on doing all of the things required to be ready and in position for the next batter. She can execute a quick systems check: How many outs? What's the score? What bases are occupied? What could the next play be? She can follow this up with a physical check: taking three steps off the base, bending her knees and dropping into a ready position—glove in front of her body with her head up.

She can control all of things listed above as well as a host of others not mentioned.

What kills high-performance is when an athlete continues to focus on, and worry about, things she can't control.

Doing so wastes energy and focus and sets an athlete up for failure. Through my experience and research, I've found that **when we focus on the things we can control, the things we can't control often take care of themselves.**

Breathe Deeply

The third internal-focused practice that showed up consistently with high-performing individuals is the use of a very specific breathing pattern called autogenic breathing.

Autogenic breathing is the athlete's lifeblood for high-performance.

When done properly, this breathing technique can slow your heart rate and respiration, lessen the trembling in your hands and arms, and restore your sense of control over yourself and the situation. This technique is one of the most valuable tools an athlete possesses.

Military personnel and law enforcement officers have been using autogenic breathing techniques for decades.

Tactical operators are taught to perform autogenic breathing while stacked outside a high-threat residence they are about to enter. It is critical that they are thinking clearly and have fine motor skills at their disposal in the event that they have to engage the threat. Autogenic breathing is also used extensively in the training of snipers. You can imagine the impact of trembling hands and rapid shallow breathing would have on a sniper's ability to hit a target from a long distance.

Autogenic breathing is part of the toolbox of the world's most elite warriors for one reason—it works.

The Law of Performance

Let's take a step backwards for a moment to discuss why there is a need for autogenic breathing at all. The value of this breathing approach can be understood more clearly when discussed in conjunction with "The Law of Diminishing Performance."

There are a number of performance laws that are very valuable for the athlete to embrace and understand. However, in the realm of high-stakes performance laws, "The Law of Diminishing Performance" reigns as king.

It is the law that states: When the stress-induced heart rate goes up, rational decision-making skills deteriorate.

Frankly, it doesn't matter how good your quarterback's arm is when he is unable to think clearly and make quick, rational decisions in the pocket. This law trumps all other performance laws when one is unable to control the physiological and psychological responses to high-stress.

And every athlete, soldier, and leader deals with high-stress environments at some point in their careers.

This law deals with those times when pressure, stress, or anxiety inhibits performance. It is when the athlete allows their anxiety to go unchecked and they move beyond the optimal arousal level for performance. It becomes the psychological and physiological recipe for an athlete to "choke."

Choking is one of those concepts that is hard to define, but you know it when you see it. It is often characterized by a progressive decline in performance from which the athlete or team can't seem to escape. Choking occurs in all sports and professions. Choking is more than making a mistake: it's feeling helpless while making mistake after mistake.

It is the defensive lineman who is called off-sides and then is called for a personal foul the very next play.

It is the basketball player who has the ball stolen from her and immediately makes a sloppy foul resulting in a 3-point play.

It is the volleyball player who misses a critical serve into the net and follows with a shanked service reception.

It is the law enforcement officer trying out for his department's S.W.A.T. team that doesn't back up his teammate entering a room in a mock warrant service, only to follow his mistake by mishandling his firearm and accidently discharging a round.

And, it is the corporate CEO who makes a large financial mistake only to follow her costly blunder by lying to the board about the extent of the damage.

One of the greatest tools for breaking this cycle is as simple as breathing. But don't confuse simple with easy; it takes some work.

Back to Breathing

The ability to take your breathing under conscious control for a short amount of time is one of the greatest keys to regaining your locus of control.

In 1954, Julian Rotter introduced the enlightening concept of locus of control. This concept addresses the extent to which people believe they have power over events and outcomes they encounter. Autogenic breathing has the potential to impact an athlete's perception of control. When you control your breathing, you reprogram your body to reduce the stress response. The manual slowing of your breathing helps to slow your respiration and regain your locus of control. As you might expect, your chances for *controlling* your anxiety, fear, and stress increase the sooner you are able to recognize that you are experiencing a stress response and take actions to control your breathing.

Autogenic Breathing: 101

Autogenic breathing is actually a very simple process.

By its nature, it must be simple, because the times it is most needed are times of high-stress and anxiety.

The technique needs to be simple because the athlete, soldier, or leader employing it is involved in a very stressful situation.

Autogenic breathing can be broken down into the following phases:

Phase I:
Inhale through the nose for a count of four. Make sure to take the breath down into your diaphragm. Do not chest breathe. Your belly should extend outward as you take in the long, slow breath.

Phase II:
Hold the breath in your belly for a count of four.

Phase III:
Exhale the breath out of your mouth for a count of four.

Phase IV:
Remain empty for a count of four.

While this technique itself is simple, it must be trained to the point where it becomes conditioned. You must train it to be your default breathing technique when stressed.

I encourage athletes to use this both in and out of the athletic realm. It is a great technique to use prior to taking an exam or giving a speech.

For college and professional athletes, I also encourage its use prior to giving interviews or speaking at a press conference. Far too many athletes have said things they wish they could take back because they were too emotionally charged to think clearly.

Autogenic Breathing under High-Stress Situations

I'll be honest: I'm terrified of flying.

I realize there is no rational reason for it, but as soon as the cabin door is secured, I break out sweating. I think part of my fear is the realization that I have to surrender all control to someone I don't even know. Regardless of why, it terrifies me.

For over an hour, I waited at my gate hoping they would eventually cancel my flight. I know that sounds crazy, but I would rather spend the night in an airport than get on the plane at that moment; the flight had been delayed due to thunderstorms and high winds in the area.

Sure enough, the announcement was made that we would begin boarding immediately. I couldn't believe it. It was still storming. Okay, it wasn't storming at that exact moment, but I was watching the news and they showed storms throughout the area. I definitely didn't want to get on that plane.

We boarded a small, regional jet. It was the type that had one row of seats on one side of the aisle and two rows of seats on the other side. Our flight time to New York, LaGuardia Airport, was two hours. Surely, I could be brave for a couple of hours. I hoped.

Not thirty minutes into the flight, I experienced the worst turbulence of my life. The plane was slammed side to side and would occasionally drop, for what felt like hundreds of feet, only to be rocked back and forth again. This had been going on for about twelve minutes at this point. I know this because I looked at my watch to determine my potential time of death when the chaos began…and I checked it once again when the pregnant woman behind me vomited into the aisle.

I was terrified. People were screaming, yes, screaming, when the plane would drop or was catapulted to the side. And, of course, there was that one guy who was also scared out of his mind, but had to mask it with "funny" comments like, "Everyone, get your hands up, we're on a rollercoaster!" or "You can't pay for this much fun!"

Everyone on the plane wanted to throw him out, but we were all too scared to let go of our armrests that we were white-knuckling. And remember the pregnant lady who puked? Well, that puke smell started wafting up the aisle and before long, two other people vomited. Then a third and a fourth. It was a flying puke fest.

Amid all of this chaos, something very odd occurred to me. Out of nowhere I thought to myself, "I truly don't know if we are going to make it through this, and since I don't have any control over how it will turn out, I might as well try autogenic breathing." I had been teaching this breathing approach for many years at this point, but I had never had to use it when I was completely terrified. I got my chance.

I closed my eyes and I started to inhale through my nose (the vomit scent still permeating the cabin, making for an overwhelming distraction). Instead of it being the smooth process that I had taught for many years, it sounded like I was trying to hyperventilate through my nose. My four second hold in the diaphragm was more like a 1.2 second hold, followed by a rapid series of outgoing breaths, like when your massage therapist tells you to exhale while she performs a series of staccato elbow thrusts on your scapula. In other words, the breathing I did initially didn't look or sound like what I had been teaching.

I kept trying. I had to regain my locus of control. After a few minutes of intense focus (a few minutes that felt like a few hours), my breathing finally resembled the autogenic breathing I had been teaching. In the process, I became more calm and clear. For the first time since I boarded that flight, I could think rationally.

This experience convinced me of the power of autogenic breathing. It took a few minutes, but I was able to regain some of my faculties and I felt that if I needed to move to assist someone or to get off the plane, I would be able to do so. This was a huge step considering the state I was in prior to starting the autogenic breathing.

ACR

1. Try some visualizing of your own. Choose an upcoming event and think of every detail, your role, and your desired outcome. Replay it exactly how you want it to go. Repeat. Repeat. Repeat. Then execute.

2. Do you have any "garbage in"? How can you change your self-talk to remove the garbage and create empowering input and output? What internal dialogue do you need to change? How do you think it will affect your external performance?

3. When do you get anxious or nervous? Before a test? Before a big game? During that big game? When your coach critiques you?

Practice the autogenic breathing technique from this chapter. Practice it again. Do it tomorrow morning. Try it when you feel anxious. Keep practicing until it feels natural.

LEADERSHIP AND HIGH-PERFORMING TEAMS

....

While a coach can suggest, cajole, threaten, and plead with an athlete to do these internal-focused practices, it is ultimately up to the athlete alone to decide the degree to which she implements them.

I have believed for a very long time, thanks to my father, that we are personally responsible, as an athlete, business person, or any professional, to bring our greatness to everything we do every day.

The practices of mental rehearsal and visualization, monitoring your self-talk, and exercising autogenic breathing are designed to help the athlete (and anyone in a high-stress situation) ensure that their capabilities exceed their limitations.

While these practices are available to anyone to stretch their capacities, only a rare few ever perfect them.

Why?

Because of the cost.

Self-discipline is the currency of excellence.

Each of these internal-focused practices requires more than most are willing to sacrifice. It is my hope that you are one of the few committed to investing in yourself and your team through self-discipline and a genuine love for your sport and your teammates. I can promise you, when you look back years from now, you won't regret the cost you paid to play.

What Do You See?

How do you view failure?

It has been my experience that high performers look at failure much differently than most people.

At the beginning of the book, I shared an anecdote about a soldier in Hawaii who approached me at the conclusion of my training and asked if they were combat ready. That was a major tipping point for me professionally. I purposely referred to it as a failure in my story because, at the time in my life when it transpired, I completely thought of it as a failure—a monumental failure, to be exact.

But it wasn't a failure at all.

At the time, I was doing the best I knew how to do. I put my heart and soul into those train-ups. I gave those soldiers the best close quarters combat techniques I possessed.

That young soldier actually did me, and those I would go on to train in the future, a great favor by having the courage to ask me such a pointed question. He changed my life in an instant. I truly wish I knew his name so I could share how his bravery made me a better instructor and set me on a path to make a difference in how people look at high-performance. I hope someday he reads one of my books and reaches out to me.

What that young man did was teach me the power of feedback.

In a simple question, he opened up a whole new world for me. I had never before thought about the mental side of the training. I wasn't the one delivering the tip of the sword, so I gave very little consideration to the dynamic situation in which it had to be accomplished. Had I not given his question the time and mental gymnastics that it deserved, I might still be looking at that day as a complete failure and I know this book would have never been written.

I now believe that with a few exceptions, there is no such thing as failure, only feedback—*if* we learn from our mistakes.

Can you fail a class or lose a game, match, or race?

Absolutely.

I can show you my transcripts to prove it. But I look at each of those examples as failures only when I haven't learned anything from them. I understand that it is difficult to see failure as feedback. Even looking at it from that perspective can bruise our egos. But you don't succeed in life or in sport without a few scars and bruises.

Too often I see students perform poorly on an exam and the first thing they want to do is forget about it. As a professor, it has always amazed me how I would offer to meet with students individually during my office hours to review their exam to help them understand where they made errors and how to correct them, and no one showed up. They were missing out on a wonderful opportunity to learn from their mistakes. The feedback was available; they just didn't want to hear it.

Many athletes do the same thing. They have a bad game and they want to move on and forget it. But the loss, while painful, can provide a wonderful education if we are willing to reflect on it and work to understand how to improve.

Too many athletes and coaches have been conditioned to fear failure.

It's understandable, right?

Winning is much more enjoyable than losing. Schools and fans want winning teams. Coaches are fired right and left if they don't produce winning teams, seasons, or individual champions.

No wonder there is an underlying aversion to failing in athletics.

Instead of treating a loss for what it is—feedback on performance and an opportunity to improve—we treat it like a sickness. Something to be avoided at all costs. That is why, as least in part, some teams and athletes approach competition as the prey.

Predator or Prey

Fear of failure impacts our inner dialogue.

This can be destructive because inner dialogue impacts our attitude and how we approach the big competition, game, or event. Consider a soccer team that is preparing for their biggest game of the season against a much higher rated team. The underdog team is at a crossroads as it begins its game preparation.

It is at this point that I will ask the team what I consider to be one of the most important questions they must answer before they begin final game preparations:

"Are you the predator or the prey?"

I want them to take a step back and reflect on their mindset. Are they focusing on the things they can't control? On things that cause anxiety? Are they afraid of failing? Or are they focused on the things that are in their zone of control? What does their inner dialogue sound like?

A predator and a prey approach a situation quite differently.

When I worked at West Point, I would often share anecdotes with cadets that soldiers had shared with me about their mindset in battle. One of my favorite examples came from a soldier who had recently returned from a combat deployment. He spoke of a lesson he had learned very quickly during his tour. It went something like this:

Imagine working your way through a cluster of houses in search of those responsible for attacking your convoy. Your team finally reaches a residence where you believe the attackers have taken shelter. Your heart races as you and your team prepare to breach the door and enter.

This soldier explained that there is a critical moment prior to the initial entry that is pivotal in a team's success or failure. It is the moment when the team collectively chooses whether they will enter as the predator or as the prey.

In the situation described above, my friend taught me that **there exists a tactical advantage to the team who enters the residence with speed, surprise, and violence of action.**

Worrying about your training and preparation at this point only leads to a prey's mindset. It will cause you to lose the aggressive momentum that is needed to overwhelm the opponent.

Worry causes hesitation, and hesitation gives your opponent the advantage.

There is a distinct difference between the attitude, actions, and, ultimately, the goal of the predator compared to that of the prey. The predator will move with a sense of confidence and a clear vision of its goal. The prey, on the other hand, will move with hesitancy and a lack of confidence.

The prey's goal is to survive while the predator's goal is to dominate the situation.

- Which mindset, that of the predator or the prey, do you think has the greatest chance of successfully negotiating the tactical situation described by the combat veteran?

- Which team, the one filled with predators or the one filled with prey, do you think will have the greatest chance of victory in the sporting arena?

Fear of failure creates a mindset that destroys high-performance. But if an athlete views losses and disappointments in terms of feedback and not failure, they move one step closer to building a mindset that facilitates growth, confidence, and a continual honing of skills. And this is precisely the mindset of a high-performer.

Self-Discipline and High-Performance

Self-discipline is the backbone that connects all the behaviors and practices throughout this book.

It's also the most elusive and deceptive of all the principles because it doesn't give you immediate feedback. You will, however, reap long-term success if you have the self-discipline to practice and master the components of high-performance decision-making.

Every decision a high performer makes—in the classroom, in the arena, or in life—is part of their success savings account.

Success or disappointment resides in the seemingly insignificant decisions we make each day.

The question you need to ask yourself on a daily basis:

"Are you making deposits or withdrawals on your personal success account?"

This question is all about counting, not costing. It is about making decisions that position you as an asset, not a liability, to yourself, your team, your family, or your school.

Imagine you have an 8 a.m. class every Monday, Wednesday, and Friday this semester. After a track meet, two states away, you return to campus at 1:30 a.m. on Wednesday. By the time you get unpacked, back to your apartment and ready for bed, it's now 2:30 a.m. You're exhausted as you set your alarm for 7:20 a.m., the absolute latest you can sleep in and still make it to your class in the science building. Sometime around 3 a.m. you actually drift off to sleep.

The minutes of the alarm clock change from 19 to 20, and you are startled awake at the ridiculously early hour of 7:20 a.m. Moment of truth. If you decide to turn the alarm off, go back to sleep and skip your class, will it make you a terrible student and ruin your entire academic career?

Nope.

What if you exercise that self-discipline we have been discussing throughout this book and pop out of bed, get dressed and head to class? Will it make you an honor student and solidify you as a stellar scholar?

Nope.

Then why are we even discussing this situation?

Simple: it's a reality check.

Most people want things to be black and white. If you want to be wealthy, do this and riches will come your way. If you want to pass this exam, study these notes. But life doesn't work that way. At least, not on the timeline most of us would choose.

But the decision to go back to sleep or to get out of bed *does matter.* That single choice may not make or break your academic career today, but that choice repeated each morning can make or break it over the long haul. One missed 8 a.m. class probably won't hurt you but six missed 8 a.m. classes most definitely will.

It is in the small, seemingly insignificant, decisions that we create our success (or our disappointment).

Take for example the swimmer who, during the off-season, has been given a workout schedule from her coach. Will skipping the 200 meters kicking drill ruin her swimming career? Will doing the 200 meters kicking drill make her faster today? No and no. But making the decision to cut corners again and again will have an impact (and not the good kind). The same goes for making the seemingly insignificant decision to not cut corners.

Each of these decisions is simple. Jeff Olson, in his powerful book, *The Slight Edge: Secret to a Successful Life*, points out that these decisions are easy to do and not to do, and therein lies the real struggle. Is it simple to cheat on the drill in the summer training regimen?

Yes.

Is it just as easy to follow exactly what the coach suggested?

Yes, again.

What this boils down to is that success is a product of self-discipline applied in an intelligent and ethical manner to the myriad decision points we have on a daily basis. I think of this approach as the athletic extension of the verse in the United States Military Academy's Cadet Prayer that states: "Make me choose the harder right instead of the easier wrong."

The Glue of Excellence

Leadership is the duct tape, the 550 paratrooper cord, and the super glue of high performing teams.

Without it, high-performance happens by accident, divine providence, or pure luck.

An intentional approach to leadership development, however, helps to ensure that teams always have a pipeline of leaders encouraging and policing the team's standards.

I have yet to work with a team where the coach has told me that their biggest problem is they have too many good leaders. I suspect I'll never hear that, and rightly so. Strong leadership throughout the entire team is required for sustainable high-performance. And developing strong leaders takes time and skill.

I'm guessing that many of you reading this book have been asked or told at some point in your athletic career to step up and be a leader. If you have ever been on the receiving end of such a statement, you know how overwhelming and frightening that charge can appear. It has been my experience in working with athletes that very few have been exposed to structured leadership programs. Unfortunately, athletes are frequently left on their own to figure it out.

Oftentimes, the extent of leadership development offered comes in the overused and misunderstood mantras such as, "Be more vocal" or "Lead from the front." I'm not sure, "Come on, guys. We can beat this team!" is really the leadership the coach was hoping for. And, what if you are not a vocal person? Surely that doesn't exclude you from the leadership club, right?

What about leading from the front? There is much more to this idea than simply standing in front of your team. Being told that you need to step up and lead is not enough direction for most athletes. That's like telling me to solve a quadratic equation without first providing any of the fundamental mathematical skills. I guarantee you would be disappointed with my answer and I would feel frustrated, lost, and defeated.

Many athletes erroneously believe that leading from the front entails being loud and obnoxious, calling out teammates who make mistakes, and taking credit for the team's success. Such behavior makes an athlete no more of a leader than the athlete that chooses to hang back in the shadows and not make any waves. Leading from the front has nothing to do with posturing and everything to do with personal accountability.

High-Performance Leadership Defined

Perhaps a starting point for better understanding the role leadership plays in a team's cohesion and, ultimately their performance, is to begin with a definition: Leadership is the activity of engaging dynamic challenges.

This definition gets its utility from the combination of two powerful concepts embedded within. The first key piece of the definition is the framing of leadership as an activity; the second is how one engages a dynamic challenge.

This definition expands the scope of who can be considered a leader. In essence, it dispels the misconception that leadership is a function of title or position. Being a senior or a team captain does not make a leader. Nor does being the star player automatically qualify you as a leader. I have witnessed many teams fall for this myth and end up wondering what went wrong.

Behaving like a leader makes you a leader. This definition classifies leadership as something every athlete on a team can exhibit. It doesn't matter if you are the top scorer, the fastest runner, or the athlete that hasn't seen a minute of playing time. **Leadership is about behavior choices.** The athlete chooses to do the things that demonstrate leadership—or they choose not to. It's that easy (and that difficult).

So, what do those leadership behaviors look like? While each group will define these behaviors for their particular tribe, I do believe that there are a few leadership behaviors that span across sports and teams of all kinds. **These universal high-performance leadership behaviors revolve around ethical decision-making and the way we treat others (dynamic challenges).**

The Golden Rule is a great starting point for all leaders. I realize such a statement sounds incredibly simplistic and possibly even naïve. However, such an approach solves a variety of problems I see leaders struggle with daily.

Consider, for a moment, how you would like to be treated by your coach and teammates. I'm guessing that you would want to be trusted, respected, and cared for (sound familiar?).

A second universal high-performance leader behavior has already been addressed in this book, but it warrants repeating here. The practice of **choosing the harder right over the easier, more comfortable wrong** is one of the most important and most powerful gifts a leader can give herself and her teammates. A leader that exhibits high levels of ethics and discipline in decision-making will not go unnoticed. Not only is the leader doing the right thing by choosing to take the high road, she is teaching leadership through her actions.

A third, powerful behavior that the most effective high-performance leaders employ is the practice of treating everyone "As if."

Several years ago a colleague shared this powerful approach with me and since then, I have witnessed many leaders utilize it with success. Such an approach to leadership entails giving each member of your team the benefit of the doubt. It allows for second chances and it shifts accountability back on the shoulders of each athlete.

Second chances separate those athletes who made an honest mistake from those who knowingly broke the rules. For instance, imagine you are a team captain and on Friday afternoon, several hours before your home basketball game, you come to find out that two of your freshmen teammates attended a party last night. You speak with your coach about the situation and you ask permission to address this matter with them in private. You have a few options of how you might approach them.

Unfortunately, the most common approach is to assume that the information you received is true and begin your conversation with your two teammates in a combative, accusatory, and angry tone. This approach rarely achieves the desired outcome which should be to ascertain the truth and, if need be, educate them on the expected behaviors.

Perhaps a more effective approach would be to take your teammates aside to tell them what you heard and then ask them about it. Treat them as if they are good, caring, and team-focused players. Maybe they respond and tell you that they did attend the party, but they didn't consume any alcohol. Maybe, and I know I'm reaching here, they really didn't understand that they weren't allowed to attend a party on the night prior to a game even if they didn't consume alcohol. Or maybe they admit they did attend (and did consume alcohol).

Regardless of whether they made an innocent mistake or not, you gave them the benefit of the doubt while educating them about future behaviors. It is at this point that the coach needs to be brought back into the mix to make a decision regarding the consequences of their actions.

Handling the situation in such a manner, however, accomplishes several important things. First, your teammates have been educated on what is correct and expected behavior. A second infraction speaks volumes about their commitment to the team and provides solid grounds for their dismissal. Second, it shifts the responsibility of following the rules back onto the teammates.

A team captain or a coach shouldn't have to carry that responsibility. You can't control others' behaviors, so you have to establish a system that makes it clear that you trust them to be a responsible and mature team member. Treating them "As If" they want to do the right thing makes uncomfortable situations a little more bearable while educating them on expected and appropriate behaviors. In order to be a truly high-performing team, every member of your tribe must embrace, understand, and adhere to these leadership behaviors.

ACR

1. What is an event in your life that you consider a failure? How could you learn from it and turn the situation into feedback?

2. How do you really approach a stressful event—as a predator or prey? What can you fix to become the predator and move away from the prey mindset?

3. What decisions are you making that affect your personal success account? Be honest with yourself.

Keep track over the next day, week, and month. What is your balance at the end? Reflect on your findings.

4. Why do you want to be a leader? Who are you leading? Create a personal leadership philosophy. Post it where you will see it often. Think about it each time you see it. Change your philosophy as your leadership abilities grow and evolve.

TIME TO TRAIN

Years ago, when I ran a martial arts academy that trained fighters, I had two signs in my gym.

One you have already been introduced to: "Check your ego at the door."

The other sign read: "Time to train."

I chose to hang the latter because I am of the belief that there comes a time to stop talking and start doing.

That time is now.

If the behaviors, practices, and examples in this book have resonated with you, give them a shot. They are only valuable when put into practice.

If you find value in this book, then please share it with a fellow athlete or a coach. If you have any suggestions for how to improve it or if you have stories or successes that you would be willing to share please reach out to me. I would love to hear your feedback and learn from you.

The older I get the more I realize how many people have played a huge role in how I look at the world. I owe a huge debt to my father, numerous coaches who have shared their wisdom with me, and to the military and law enforcement officers who took me in as a civilian and shared so many lessons that I use on a daily basis. Each of them helped to expand and shape the lens through which I gaze at life.

Ralph Waldo Emerson once wrote, "The mind, once stretched by a new idea, never returns to its original dimensions."

High performers constantly seek opportunities to grow.

Do you?

Dr. Jason Winkle is the founder and CEO of WinkleCorp, a leadership development consultancy, and President of WinkleAthlete, a player and team development organization for athletes and coaches.

He also serves as Associate Dean in the College of Nursing, Health, & Human Services at Indiana State University.

Dr. Winkle is a former faculty member at the United States Military Academy at West Point, New York. He is a sought-after speaker, consultant, and coach. He lives in Indiana with his family.

JOIN THE INSURGENCY

Interested in finding more high-impact books just like this one? Check out **Insurgent Publishing**: a boutique, publishing company that produces hard-hitting nonfiction for the creative outliers of the world.

Join the Insurgency to receive:

1. Early access to all our products

2. Behind the scenes looks at current and future projects

3. Access to exclusive bonus material including interviews with authors, designers and much more.

Join the Insurgency today:

www.**InsurgentPublishing**.com/**join**

CPSIA information can be obtained at www.ICGtesting.com
Printed in the USA
LVOW11s1345271014

410680LV00001B/143/P